Someone to Love

A PLAYWRIGHT BY
MYRA L. TURNAGE

FULL CIRCLE PUBLISHING
BILOXI, MS

Full Circle Publishing
PO Box 8549
Biloxi, MS 39535

Editing by Full Circle Publishing & Julie Keene
Manufactured in the United States of America

ISBN-13: 978-0692910047 (Full Circle Publishing)
ISBN-10: 0692910042

www.juliekeene.com

~

Someone to Love is dedicated to all those who have fought for self-preservation to find inner peace. There is beauty found in the realization of knowing that the greatest love we can give to someone comes from a heart filled with a greater God given love that we have for ourselves.

~

SOMEONE TO LOVE

Dontae had not seen Monique in months. He was not sure if she even wanted to see him. But he had to bite the bullet and be the standup guy he should have been a long time ago. Besides, how old was Olivia now? At least eighteen months and he had not even laid eyes on his own flesh and blood.

Dontae: *(Rapping on the door old school or should I say High School! Dun dun da dun dun dun dun)* Yea, who else but me Monique!!

Monique*: (Comes to the door with a smirk on her face and opens the door)* So, you still think you are so important that I would automatically know it was you?

Dontae: And you didn't?

Monique*: (Now with a big grin and open arms)* Whatever! *(Hugging each other)* Where you been all my life? I should be going up side you head for not calling, not coming around or nothing! I mean!?!?

Dontae*: (Now inside Monique's modest apartment)* Well, you know when I told you I had to get away to get myself straight, I meant that. I know I should have called or something but I didn't want to give myself any excuse to slip. And don't even mention the fact that a lot of people wanted my head on a platter.

Monique: So are you saying you are straight now?

Dontae: Better.

Monique: Dontae are you still using or not? And I certainly don't need no trouble coming around here because of some mess you got over your head. You know it's not just about me anymore. My baby means everything to me. I love you dearly and I want you in our lives but not if means trouble. Besides, you haven't been around all this time. I can certainly get along without you. And...

Dontae: Baby slow down! Woman! Give a dude a break!

Monique: A break?

Dontae: Monique, look, I'm better. I don't owe nobody nothing. Nobody's gonna be coming around here looking for me. I wouldn't do that to you and the baby! (*The beautiful angel runs into the room. Monique picks up her precious baby girl.*)

Monique: Olivia (*The three hug*)

Dontae: You know, we are all we've got.

The next couple of weeks, Dontae and Monique spend a lot of time together, catching up, getting reacquainted, grilling, and going down the soul train line (BRICK HOUSE). Dontae is bonding with Olivia. He's not so bad at the babysitting thing either.

ONE MONTH LATER

Olivia looks out the window of her apartment. She could recognize the sound of Dontae's old clunker anywhere. Dontae is shaking hands with some dude. Monique thinks she recognizes him but can't quite place him.

Dontae: *(Walks in with champagne and roses in tow. So excited, he picks up Monique as though she is a little rag doll)* I got it! I got it! I got the job! You are looking at the newest member of Facilities Management at Huff Spalding Children's Medical Center. I am a working man now. I'm legit. A working man.

Monique: Way da go!
(They open up the champagne)

Monique: To you!

Dontae: Yea to Me!

Later the two are sitting in front of the tube catching "Criminal Minds". Dontae reaches inside his pocket and brings out a joint.

Monique: Donte don't start that up in here!

Dontae: Just a little weed.

Monique: But Olivia.

Dontae: Well you won't have to worry about her waking up the rest of the night.

Monique: *(Slapping Dontae on the shoulder)* This isn't funny.

Dontae: Sounds like you need this more than I do.

They smoke the joint. The next day Monique finds herself in the Nurse's station taking off orders. Dr. Farrington walks up.

Dr. Farrington: Who is taking care of Mr. Thompson in bed 5?

Monique: He's mine.

Dr. Farrington: Can I see you in the conference room?

(They go into the conference room which is conveniently empty.)

Dr. Farrington: (*With frustration in his voice*) After midnight last night I had 10 phone calls. All of them were from you, Monique. Things have really gotten out of hand.

Monique: If you had picked up the first time you would have had only one phone call after midnight last night. At least only one from me.

Dr. Farrington: You know it's not that simple.

Monique: It used to be. You used to call me all the time in the night. At least when you were not lying in bed beside me.

Dr. Farrington: Monique, I thought we had gotten this all behind us. We agreed that it is best that we call it quits and just be friends.

Monique: Well, friends with benefits just doesn't work for me anymore. That's just difficult to do when you're in love with some who you cannot have. But you wouldn't know anything about that, huh?

Dr. Farrington: You know I can't divorce Patricia right now. With all she is going through. Leave her while she is going through chemo? I couldn't do that to her. Besides the kids they would never forgive me.

Monique: We've been seeing each other five years now, David. Patricia started chemo only six months ago. And no, I don't expect you to divorce your wife. I stopped believing that a long time ago.

Dr. Farrington: Is that why you decided to start your family without me? Cheating on me?

Monique: Cheating on you? You have some nerve! You are a married man. How can I cheat on you? Well I guess I have to ask myself who is the fool here?

Dr. Farrington: *(Putting his arms around Monique and looking straight into her eyes)* Please believe me. I love you and you are no fool for loving me. We love each other and that we cannot deny. Patricia filed for divorce two months before she got her diagnosis. If she had not gotten sick we would already be divorced and you and I would be together. You know that baby.

Monique: I have to go. I have work to do.

Dr. Farrington: Are you ever going to tell me who Olivia's father is?

Monique: Thanks to good old DNA you are certain she is not yours.

Dr. Farrington: I had to be certain.

Monique: You know I became pregnant last year during our break. Four months David. We were apart. I never tried to pass her off as yours. You still tested her without my permission.

Dr. Farrington: I had to be certain. I guess I wanted so badly for her to be mine. I love you that much Monique.

Monique: Like I said, I have work to do. *(Monique walks out of the conference room.)*

OVERHEAD PAGE: Dr. David Farrington please call 82213. 82213 Dr. Farrington please call 82213

Monique goes into an empty patient room. She takes out a bottle of Xanax, prescribed by no other than the good Dr. David Farrington, leans over the sink and pops two at a time and looks in the mirror.

Monique: God I hope I can make the next two hours of my shift.

Monique reports off duty, makes it through traffic, reaches her apartment and manages to start dinner. She sees a band of ants on the counter.

Monique: Dag, I've told Dontae over and over to wipe the counter after he puts sugar in his coffee.
Monique opens the cabinet over the refrigerator to find bug spray. To her surprise and disgust behind the bug sprays she finds a bag of white powder.

Monique: No way Dontae!

His timing is perfect. Dontae walks through the front door. Monique starts spraying Dontae...in the face, everywhere. Trying to get away and calm her down he runs into the kitchen. Bad idea. Monique picks up a butchers knife.

Dontae: Monique! Monique! (He is able to pen her against the fridge and get the knife out of her hand. He sees the bag of goods on the counter.)

Dontae: Monique, I'm sorry! It's not what you think! I am not using. I'm not using! I'm not using!

Monique: It's in my house! What about Olivia? Did you even think about her? Of course not just yourself!

Dontae: Calm down, please? When I first came into town I got this just as leverage. I didn't know how long before I would find work. For distribution only. Just in case I needed some cash. I swear. I promise. I swear.

Monique: So not using but pushing. I should SLICE you!

TWO MONTHS LATER

Dontae and Monique arrive in style at the Marriot Downtown. They both look beautiful. They find themselves at the punch bowl. Each checking out the crowd. Monique notices Dr. Farrington. Waiting for some kind of sign from Monique that it is ok to join her and the gentleman she is with, his impatience wins over. He starts to walk over, but is joined by his escort. They reach the couple together.

Dr. Farrington: Monique you look beautiful.

Monique: So do you and Patricia. Hi Patricia. It's good to see you out and about.

Patricia: *(Waves only)*

Dr. Farrington: So is this Olivia's...

Monique: Uncle. Olivia's Uncle. My brother. My brother from the same mother and same father.

After a little bit of dancing and a whole lot of drinking, Monique finds herself alone long enough to pop a couple of Xanax. Back at the apartment Monique stumbles onto the sofa. Dontae is both shocked and afraid at what he is witnessing. He knew he and his sister had addictive behaviors but up to this point he thought Monique's was limited to designer shoes and Starbucks.

Dontae: Monique, so how long have you been seeing the good doctor? Is he Olivia's father?

Monique: Mind your own business.

Dontae: I have been. But after seeing you popping pills and drinking like there was some kind of liquor famine on the way I think I need to pry a little bit you think? *(Goes to bed)*

Monique: *(Leaving a message for the good old doctor)* Call me

TEXT: Monique it's over. I'm sorry it's over. I have to think about my family. Please know that I will always love you.

THE NEXT MORNING

Dontae walks into the living room to find his sister still slumped on the sofa just where he left her.

Dontae: Monique, hey sleeping beauty. Wake up, we need to talk about this, all that happened last night and the stuff you are going through.

Dontae: Monique! Monique! Baby wake up*! (He notices the glass of vodka, the Xanax and bag of powder on the end table.)*

Dontae: Monique! Oh my God! What have I done??!! *(He tries to wake his beloved sister.)* What have I done??!! *(The paramedics come and go, taking away his beloved sister.)*

Dontae: *(Crying in the dark)* God I have no one! No one! No one to love me! No one to love!

The Home going service was two days later. Dontae and Olivia embracing as they watched their beloved body lower into the earth and they cast their eyes to the sky as her spirit drifted away just like a vapor from their tears.

~ *11* ~

Dontae packs the last of Monique's things. He finds two envelopes tucked inside a PDR that sits on her desk. He opens the first. Metropolitan DNA Diagnostic Testing Center. DAVID FARRINGTON TO OLIVIA SIMPSON; 99.99% NOT THE FATHER.
Second envelope: Georgia Fertility Clinics of America. IN VITRO FERTILIZATION; POSITIVE PREGNANCY; DONOR UNDISCLOSED.

Dontae: Dr. Farrington not the daddy. That's just like my sister. Doing it on her own. I guess it would be useless trying to find any other next of kin. Monique what were you thinking? Taking that dust. You never even had a hit of dust in life before. Not ever.

Dontae spends the next several weeks trying to figure out how to work an eighteen month old baby girl into his life. Having no prior experience, this would be a tough one. It was just the two, Dontae and Monique growing up along with their mom. Dad, well who was he anyway? Mom had no real family to speak of. At least none she thought enough of to share with Monique and Dontae.

Dontae finds himself back at work. He avoids conversation with most of his co-workers. I guess the pain of having lost his only family coupled with the guilt of feeling Monique's death was all his fault was much too horrible to bear or share with anyone what he was going through.

Dontae: Why didn't I just stay out of her life? *(He slams his locker door with disgust.)*

Dontae: Hi Beverly don't mind me. I'm just kinda out there.

Beverly: *(One of the newly hired technicians)* No, everyone's entitled to have a rough one.

Dontae: (*Looking lost*) Yea

Beverly: Girl problems?

Dontae: Like you wouldn't believe. And if I'm not there to pick her up in about fifteen minutes I am going to be in deep trouble.

Beverly: One of those types?

Dontae: You got it. One of those types.

Beverly: Well why don't you bring her out and meet up with me and some of the guys after work? We are getting together at SHOUT around eight.

Dontae: Maybe next time. *(He looks at his watch and walks away.)*

Dontae is lucky. The fact that the hospital has a daycare for children of employees has been a blessing from the skies. He walks in, greets the staff and heads straight for Olivia.

Olivia: *(Arms open wide and reaching out for her uncle)* Don Don!

Dontae gathers up Olivia and heads for the door. All the mothers are watching as some whisper, while others intentionally want him to hear their comments.

Lady: I think that is so sexy.

Dontae: *(Not cracking a smile and not wanting to be bothered or cordial)* You should see me cleaning poop and trying to make pancakes. At the same time.
(The women laugh)

Lady: Gross!

Dontae: Ladies, have a good evening *(Although his facial expression doesn't show an ounce of sincerity.)*

Lady: Don't take it out on us. You the daddy, you're supposed to do your part!

Dontae: Yea.

Dontae finds himself over the next few months trying to be a good uncle to his niece. He goes to work, picks up Olivia, comes home, feeds Olivia, puts her to bed and tries not to smoke weed, drink alcohol, or cuss. All of this trying is driving him crazy but he is determined he won't fall off the wagon. He feels he owes this much to both Monique and Olivia.

The holidays come and go...Halloween, Thanksgiving and even Christmas. Dontae just cruises through. No celebrating. No trick or treating. No Thanksgiving dinner. No Christmas gifts. The day after Christmas Dontae is slumped on the sofa when he hears a little boy on TV say, "Happy Birthday Baby Jesus!" He starts to cry.

Dontae: I don't even know when your birthday is! What kind of brother was I Monique? What am I doing with your child?!

Dontae goes into the bedroom and opens the dresser drawer. He takes out some paper work.
ARTIFICIAL INSEMINATION POSITIVE,
APPROXIMATELY 12 WEEKS. He does the math.

Dontae: That means you were probably born in January. That's it...New Year's Day. That's your birthday, New Year's Day.

Seven days later Dontae brings Olivia into the kitchen. They finish dinner.

Dontae: Olivia look what Don Don has for you. *(He sits the giant pink cupcake on the table and tops it with 2 yellow candles.)*

Dontae: Olivia blow out the candles. Oh first make a wish. *(He closes his eyes, Olivia closes her eyes.)* Open your eyes. Now blow out the candles.

Olivia: SHHHHHhhhhhhhhhhhhh! *(Blowing out the candles)* Yeaaaaaaaaaaaaaa!

Dontae: Happy Birthday Olivia

Olivia: *(Embraces her uncles face)* Don Don.

Dontae: Happy New Year (*One tear drop falls*)

Olivia: *(Still embracing his face)* Don Don!

Dontae: Nothings on this tube! (*He throws the remote on the sofa beside him then picks up the phone*).The door will be open, I'll be in the shower.

A short while later in walks...let's call her Nicky. In walks Nicky. She locks the door behind her, throws her purse on the sofa and heads for the shower. A while later Dontae hears noise out front. He stops his carrying on to investigate. He puts on his sweats, walks out front, pops on the light. Olivia is lying on the sofa, eyes closed, with what appears to be white powder on her face!

Dontae: (*Rushing to her side*) Olivia! Olivia! (*He shakes her and screams out her name*) Olivia! Olivia! This can't be happening!

The night of Monique's death flashes before his eyes. He sees Nicky's open purse on the sofa. By this time Nicky has made it to his side.

Nicky: What's going on? (*Notices Olivia*) A kid?

Dontae: Where do you get off bringing drugs into my house?!?! You know I don't do that no more! Olivia! Olivia! I'm calling 911!

Olivia wakes up!

Olivia: *(Crying)* Don Don!

Dontae: (*Kissing her face*) You're ok Olivia. *(Just now he notices the sweet powder he just kissed from her face)* It's sugar! It's powdered sugar!

Nicky: I guess she got into my powdered doughnuts. Hey! You didn't tell me you had a kid!

Dontae: Get out! Get out! Get out!

Nicky: Where's my money plus cab fare?!!

Dontae shoves Nicky out the door and slams it shut. He rushes back to Olivia. He grabs her into his arms.)

Dontae: Oh my precious, I am so sorry. I am so sorry! *(He sobs.)*

Olivia: Don Don.

THE NEXT MORNING
HEAVEN'S HOUSE ADOPTION AGENCY AND
FOSTER CARE

Dontae: Can you possibly help me? Well, I should say help this child? I can't possibly continue to take care of her. Rather continue to wreck her life.

Counselor: What do you mean? Wreck her life?

Dontae: She needs someone who can take care of her, someone to love her the right way. That just ain't me. (*Dontae sits Olivia on the counselor's desk.*) Please help this child. (*He walks away, just like that. Looking into Olivia's big brown eyes, he rushes away just like that.*)

Counselor: Sir! Sir! You can't just leave this child! Sir!

The next few days are awful for Dontae. Filled with guilt and shame, he can't sleep. Every time he closes his eyes, he sees Olivia staring him in the face. Dontae lays in bed trying to sleep. Memories of his childhood with Monique haunt him. The fun they had playing and laughing all day. Summers jumping rope and playing hide and go seek. He can just hear Monique's voice after she gives him the last dime out of her pocket to buy a gumball "Don't say I never gave you nothing, I gave you all I had. I gave you all I had. I gave you all I had."

Dontae: *(Crying out in the dark)* Please forgive me!

As soon as the doors open at Heavens House, Dontae is there.

Dontae: (*Talking to the woman at the front desk*) I'm here for the little girl I brought in yesterday.

Woman: Yesterday?

Dontae doesn't wait for any further communication but instead barges through the door behind which he expects to find Olivia. He is correct. Olivia is asleep alone in a small cramped looking bed. Dontae picks up Olivia and looks into her sleepy eyes.

Dontae: Olivia please forgive me. Don Don is here for you.

Olivia: *(Looking back at him as though she understands and has already forgiven him)* Don Don

Dontae walks straight past the woman at the front desk

Woman: You can't just take that child out of here! Sir! Sir!

Now that he has his beloved Olivia back safe and sound he can finally rest at night. He is lying in bed when he hears someone knocking on the door.

Nicky: It's Nicky! You owe me! (*Knock knock*). And no kids this time! *(Knock knock)*

Dontae: Go away! Please?!

Nicky: How about a free one! (*Knock knock*).

Dontae stumbles out of bed, opens the bedside table drawer full of plenty of condoms and stumbles to the front door and snatches Nicky inside

FIVE YEARS LATER

Olivia is running around in the back yard, blowing bubbles. Dontae joins her with a bottle of bubbles of his own. The pair seem so happy. They have come a long way over the past five years. Dontae knows he has done the right thing by adopting Olivia.

Olivia: Don Don, when are we going to pick up my costume for the Father/Daughter Dance?

Dontae: Let's go inside and go on line and look at some costumes.

They go to Olivia's room. The walls are decorated with her favorite girl singers: Janet, Mariah, Cher, Mary J. Blige, etc.

Dontae: I have come up with a few famous couples I think you might like.

Olivia: Who? Who?

Dontae: (*With a silly look on his face*) How about Mickey and Minnie?

Olivia: Everyone will have that! Not that!

Dontae: How about Tom and Jerry?

Olivia: Don Don.

Dontae: Heckel and Jeckel?

Olivia: Ha Ha!

Dontae: Frick and Frack, Sears and Roebuck?

Olivia: No silly!

Dontae: Mack and Cheese, Ricky and Lucy? Fred and Ethel?

Olivia: Ha Ha!

Dontae: Fred and Lamont?

Olivia: No No!

Dontae: Dunk and doughnuts? Batman and Robin?

Olivia: (*Beginning to look a little disappointed*) Are we going to find something good?

Dontae: (*Pulls a box from under the bed and flings out a long black wig*) How about...

Olivia: Yes! Sonny and Cher! Sonny and Cher!

Dontae: You got it!

Olivia: OK Daddy! This time I get to be Cher!

Dontae: Ahhh...

Olivia: I GOT YO BABE! I GOT YOU BABE!

They both laugh and laugh and laugh, avoiding the fact that for the first time ever Olivia just called him DAD

Olivia: Don Don, can I call you Dad? Do I have to keep calling you Don Don? All the other kids have Mom's and Dad's.

Dontae: Well this isn't called Daughter and Don Don Dance is it?

It hit Dontae like a ton of bricks. He didn't really pay attention to the fact that Olivia has never called him Uncle. Always Don Don. Or has Dontae just been in denial? Dontae, thinking to himself, "She believes I am her Father. She would hate me if she knew I killed her mother. Because of me this precious little girl doesn't have a mother.

Olivia: Why don't I have a Mother? Why did she leave us? Did she die? Is she in heaven?
(A tear drops from Dontae's eyes.)

Dontae: *(Still tearful)* Yes you can call me Daddy. *(Knowing that someday he will have to tell Olivia the truth, today just isn't that day.)*

Olivia: *(Wipes the tear from his face)* It's OK Daddy.

Sonny and Cher are a hit at the Dance

Knowing she will be late for school and that Dontae would soon be calling her downstairs if she doesn't make an appearance soon, Olivia runs down stairs to find her dad frying eggs and toast popping from the toaster.

Olivia: *(Kissing her dad on the forehead, she opens the fridge and grabs a cup of yogurt.)* How do you live on that stuff?

Dontae: Man cannot live on yogurt alone.

Olivia: But high cholesterol can surely send man to an early grave. And you just better not be going anywhere before you help me pick out my prom dress.

Dontae: Meet me at Phoebes' at seven tonight.

Olivia: Phoebes? Now that's what I'm talking about! Boutique! That's my dad!

Dontae: That's my girl!

Olivia, as beautiful as a gazelle rushes out the door. Later, about half way through his work day, Dontae is busy checking the main computer in the nurse's station when Dr. Sharon Roberson walks up and stands over him.

Dr. Roberson: I need this computer.

Dontae: (*Looking up*) And I would guess you need it to be working.

Dr. Roberson picks up a patients chart and ignores Dontae's comeback.

Dontae: (*Talking out loud to himself*) These docs, always looking down at guys like me. If she wasn't my doctor I would remind her that she is only human just like the rest of us. But since I am depending on her to check my cholesterol and a few other things I guess I should be nice. She probably doesn't even know I am her patient.

Dontae diligently continues working on the computer. Dr. Roberson stands up and places the chart back on the cart.

Dr. Roberson: (*Flashing her beautiful smile*) Mr. Bonneville I will see you in my office on Friday. (*The doctor leaves the nurses station.*)

Later that evening Dontae walks into Phoebes. Phoebe greets him with a smile. She offers him a bottle of water.

He declines but instead sits and waits for his daughter. Half an hour has passed and still no Olivia...no phone call, no text, no nothing. He calls her of course and after no answer, he texts. After about forty-five minutes of waiting in frustration and worry he leaves the boutique.

Back at the apartment Dontae sits on the sofa flipping through channel after channel on the TV.

Dontae: Where is she? God where is she?

Dontae hears a car door slam. He walks over to the window and see some guy pushing his beloved daughter up against his car. He opens the window. To his surprise he can hear the guy saying:

Guy: At least let me gun you.

Guy: Come on let me give you a shot gun! *(He puts his mouth over her nose and guns her.)*

All hell breaks loose. Dontae rushes outside.

Dontae: *(Pulling the guy off Olivia)* What are you doing to my daughter??!! What do you think you're doing??!!

Olivia: Don Don!! Daddy!!

Dontae throws the guy to the ground, punching and beating and kicking and punching and beating and beating and beating...

Dontae: You are wrong for this!

Olivia: Daddy, No! Please stop!!

He pushes Olivia to the ground and continues beating this guy. The terror of that awful night when he found Monique slumped on the sofa came rushing back in a flash before his face. He could only see the lifeless body of his beloved sister as the paramedics took her away. Somehow he must have thought if he pounded this guy enough Monique would come back to him.

Olivia: Daddy stop! Please you are killing him! I don't want you to go to jail for murder! If you do I'll have no one! (*Sobbing*) No one!

Dontae comes to his senses, grabs Olivia by the arm and drags her inside. Once inside Olivia runs upstairs, sobbing.

Dontae: I waited for you, so that's what you've been doing? Smoking dope? Getting high? Making a fool out of me? And a doped up whore of yourself? Let me tell you about getting high!

2:00 A.M.

Dontae: (*Staring at the ceiling*) God.

His entire life with Olivia flashes before his face, nights putting her to sleep as a baby, kissing her boo-boo when she fell on the playground, birthday parties, blowing out candles, blowing bubbles, graduation from kindergarten, graduation from grade school, trying to explain the menstrual cycle, the birds and the bees, remembering!!!!!!!!!!!!!! I GOT YOU BABE, I GOT YOU BABE...

Olivia: Sobbing...

Remembering all the fun times she's had with her dad, all the tickles, letting her make up his face, teaching her times tables, teaching her to swim, letting her have sleep overs, showing her how to play SPADES, remembering!!!!!!!!!!!!!! I GOT YOU BABE, I GOT YOU BABE...

Dontae: (*Knocking on the door*) You up? Come on I know you can't sleep either. I'm sorry. I am so sorry.

Olivia: I'm sorry! Daddy I don't do dope! I don't do no drugs. That was the first time. I promise that was the first time. My friends have been trying to get me to try for the longest time. That was the first time. I don't do no dope.

Dontae: Please, promise you won't ever do that again! Promise me. I won't lose you too, not over no drugs. We've talked about this so many times.

Olivia: I promise. I won't.

Dontae: We need to talk.

Dontae spends the next several hours explaining to Olivia how he used to do drugs, how he was strung out, how he pushed drugs, sold to young people, old people he didn't care as long as he made enough money to keep his high going. Olivia listening with disbelief. He explained how he finally hit rock bottom, lost everything, and even missed the home going service of his own mother because he was estranged from his only family...Monique. Yes, his sister, Monique.

Dontae: I got clean and came home to my sister... only.................. (*Explaining that night was the hardest thing Dontae ever had to do in his entire life.*)

Olivia: My mother, you murdered my mother! If you had stayed away, I would still have my mother! What kind of monster are you??!!

Olivia tore into Dontae with rage. She pounded into his chest until she was out of breath. Dontae took it because he believed he deserved it. They both sat in the dark embraced arm-in-arm, crying.

For the next several days Dontae and Olivia did not speak. They really had no idea what to say to each other.

DR. ROBERSON'S OFFICE

Dontae reaches the office tower and makes his way to Dr. Roberson's office. He is pleased that the wait is not long.

Dr. Roberson: Hello Mr. Bonneville.

Donte: Hello doctor.

Dr. Roberson completes her physical exam, orders some lab work and instructs Mr. Bonneville to wait for her in the conference room. After reviewing everything, she meets her patient in the conference room.

Dr. Roberson: I am happy to report another clean bill of health.

Dontae: Thank God. I guess I gave up the good life just in time.

Dr. Roberson: *(Knowing Dontae's' medical, social and drug history)* Yes, good health is something we are blessed to have. Keep up the good work.

Dontae: I will do my best. Lately that has not been so easy.

Dr. Roberson: Oh, is there anything I can help you with?

Dontae: Not unless you also specialize as a head shrink!

Dr. Roberson: No but I do know a few and I am a good listener.

Dontae begins telling Dr. Roberson about his troubles with his daughter and the whole sad story of the tragic death of his sister, Monique. Dr. Roberson empathizes with Dontae.

Dr. Roberson: Mr. Bonneville, you know guilt is a terrible burden to bear. At some point you are going to have to deal with this. I suggest you start right away. Here is the number of some of my fellow colleagues. I highly recommend that you contact someone soon. Your mental and emotional health is just as important as you physical health. Please don't hesitate to call me if you ever just need to talk.

Dontae: (*Places the business card in his pocket*) A shrink! Thanks doc I'll see you back here in a year. A whole year, that's a long time to have to wait to see you again.

Dr. Roberson smiles as she thinks to herself, is he flirting with me? Naa...

Dontae leaves the office. On his way home, driving in somewhat of a daze, he thinks about the conversation he had with Dr. Roberson. He was surprised at how easy it was to open up to her. She made him feel comfortable.

Dontae: I think she really cares about my well-being and not just the fat check she will be getting from my insurance company. Man, thanks for insurance. (*He laughs out loud.*)

(*Still thinking out loud*) What a fine woman, that Doc. I wonder what a man has to do to get a house call from you. Who am I kidding? I wouldn't stand a chance with a woman like that. Heck, I ain't fit for no woman. I ain't fit for nothing. (*Dontae pounds the stirring wheel.*)

Dontae spends the next few days going to work, some bar hopping, picking fights at the pool hall, fights he has no doubt he will win. His biggest temptation is "the bottle" calling him at every turn.

Dontae walks into the apartment. It's obvious that Olivia is in her room. He gets a bucket of ice and goes into his bedroom. A bottle of Crown Royal Black and Jack Daniel is tucked under his arm. He lays across the bed and pours it over rocks.

Dontae: Sixteen years sober and I find myself right back here. Well, Jack, you found me! You ain't been nowhere. You just been sittin' back waiting for me to mess up.
(The phone rings.)

Dontae: *(Picks up the phone.)* Monique!! *(Dial Tone)*
Dontae gets out of bed and falls on his knees.

Dontae: Father God please hear me, please forgive me for all the wrong that I have done. Please take me back. Please make me fit again. Make me fit to be a real man. Make me fit to be a father to my little girl. Please God!
Dontae walks over to Olivia's room. Knock! Knock! She opens the door then goes back and sits on her bed. Dontae walks over and sits beside her.

Dontae: Baby, I know I've done wrong by you. I know I don't deserve your trust or love for what I've done and in keeping this from you all these years. Please forgive me. I can't go on without you. Without you I have no one.

Maybe I don't deserve anyone. I guess I always knew that a gift like you was more than I ever deserved. Please forgive me.

Olivia: If you would stop talkin'! Daddy I forgive you. I love you. You are the greatest. I cannot imagine my life without you in it. Hearing about my mom was hard. No lie, I wanted you to just go away and let my mother come back in your place. I know that is impossible. I have you and that is a God given gift that I will forever be grateful. My mother made a choice. We won't ever know if her death was intentional or accidental but we do know that she made a choice to take drugs. Her death was not your fault. I forgive you. You need to forgive yourself, Daddy. Daddy, do you know that for the past four years when I blow out my birthday candles my wish is that you will find someone special to love? You deserve that. I know you love me and I will always be here but you need someone to love.

Dontae: I am not fit for anyone

Olivia: Would you please shut up! You are an awesome man. Blessed is the woman who gets you. Now get out of my room. We have a prom dress to pick out tomorrow.

Dontae goes back to his room gets the Crown Royal and Jack. He pours it down the sink.

Dontae: So long!

Back in his room, he picks up the phone.

Dontae: Hey! You feel like listening to me talk?

In his car - *MAXWELL - I can let my whole life pass me by or I can get down and try, work it all out this lifetime, lifetime.*

Dr. Roberson meets him at the door - *I can let my whole life pass me by or I can get down and try, work it all out this life time, work it all out this time, lifetime, lifetime. That's some good loving right there.*

TWO WEEKS LATER

Dontae and Sharon are sitting on the sofa when the doorbell rings. Its Olivia's date. Dontae greets him then goes to Olivia's door and escorts her out. Wearing a beautiful red gown, she is a vision to behold.

Dontae: You two have a great time. (*He hugs Olivia and whispers in her ear*) I'll be waiting up!

Olivia: Don't you dare! *(The couple leaves)*

Dontae: My how time flies!

Sharon: I know, next she'll be getting married

Dontae: I can't even think about that! Right now all I want to think about is me and you.
WELLLLLLLLLLLLLLLLLLLLL!!!!

The guests stood as they watched the beautiful bride approach her groom. What a vision in white. The bride and groom exchange vows and rings. Finally the minister says...........

Minister: *I NOW PRONOUNCE YOU MAN AND WIFE. I PRESENT TO YOU MR. AND MRS. DONTAE BONNEVILLE!!!!!!!!!!! YOU MAY KISS YOUR BRIDE!*

THE END

Someone to love, someone to trust, someone to hold, someone to know. You gave me someone. Thank you!

Celebrate good times, come on!

ABOUT THE AUTHOR – *Myra L. Turnage*

Author Myra L. Turnage has found that sharing her life experience as well as her hopes and dreams with others has given her a greater senses of connection with the universe. The author has received formal education in Healthcare Sciences and the Leadership arena. Ambition and drive have not been lacking. However, she is not unfamiliar with the many nuances that come along with growing up in a one parent home. She knows firsthand that motivation, dedication, drive, and putting into action the work needed to receive desired results are all paramount. She has an unfailing belief that faith in her Higher Power to direct her path has given her a life that otherwise would not have been realized.

www.ingramcontent.com/pod-product-compliance
Lightning Source LLC
Chambersburg PA
CBHW061757040426
42447CB00011B/2350